COMMUNAL SOCIETIES IN AMERICA
AN AMS REPRINT SERIES

SHAKER MUSIC.

AMS PRESS
NEW YORK

Library of Congress Cataloging in Publication Data

[Evans, Frederick William] 1808–1893, comp.
  Shaker music.

  (Communal societies in America)
  1. Shakers—Hymns.   I.   Title.
M2131.S4E7 1974   783.9'52   72-2988
ISBN 0-404-10750-8

Reprinted from the edition of 1875, Albany
First AMS edition published in 1974
Manufactured in the United States of America

AMS PRESS INC.
NEW YORK, N.Y. 10003

SHAKER MUSIC.

INSPIRATIONAL HYMNS AND MELODIES

ILLLUSTRATIVE OF THE

Resurrection Life and Testimony

OF THE

SHAKERS.

"AND THE COMMON PEOPLE HEAR THEM GLADLY."

ALBANY, N. Y.
WEED, PARSONS AND COMPANY, PUBLISHERS.
1875.

PREFACE.

THE Gift of Songs has been much sought and liberally obtained by the People, whose name these Hymns and Melodies bear. They are, without exception, the product of young Brethren and Sisters of the Order, who, having had no scientific, musical education, have, in their arrangement — poetical and musical — chiefly relied upon the teachings of the Spirit. Conscious of their *scientific* imperfections, they go to the public for what they are — the simple offering of a simple people.

We claim that the words and music are not *all* of Earth nor *all* of Heaven — simply inspirational gifts, appropriate to, and illustrative of, the life and testimony of Believers in Christ's First and Second Appearing, which find continual use in their sacred worship, wherein are seen Virgins rejoicing in the dance, both men and women together.

With this apology to Science and Art, we rest them upon their own merits, with those who love sincerity and beauty for their own sake.

We invite all interested to subscribe for the SHAKER AND SHAKERESS, in which may be found a continuation of the same Gift of Songs.

Price of SHAKER AND SHAKERESS, 60 cents per annum.

MT. LEBANON, COL. CO., N. Y.

SHAKER MUSIC.

CHRISTMAS OFFERING.

MT. LEBANON, N. Y.

p 1. Sweet - est mu - sic soft - ly steal - ing O'er our hearts in tune - ful chime, Shall, in joy - ous notes re - veal - ing,
f 2. Wake we now to joy and glad - ness, Christ the Sav - iour we have found; Ban - ish from our hearts all sad - ness,

Swell the song of old - en time. When the morn - ing star was beaming, An - gels sang of peace and love;
And in deeds of love a - bound. Now the fount of good un - seal - ing, Let us all our souls up - fill;

Ma - ny souls a-woke from dreaming, Hail'd the light from Heaven above. Gladsome sound we ech-o still, *p* Peace on earth, to all good will.
And, in kind-ly Christian feeling, Breathe sweet peace and speak good will. Gladsome sound we ech-o still, Peace on earth, to all good will.

BEAMS OF LIGHT.

MT. LEBANON, N. Y.

1. When the glo-ry of light beams o-ver our way, From bright souls in regions a-bove; The forms of the near, the true and the dear,

Who've pass'd from our sight, ere the day turn'd to night, Are seen flit-ting round us in love.

2.
And when we are weary and worn with life-toil,
We feel their soft presence in peace,
They brighten the hours, which ever are ours,
To rightly improve, as onward we move,
To the land where sorrow will cease.

3.
'Tis thus we are strengthened to journey below,
And bear with true pleasure each care,
For bright is the thought, with happiness fraught,
Of communion sweet, when the hours shall fleet,
That hold us earth-labor to share.

4.
O, gladly we walk by the faith of to-day,
And banish all darkness of mind,
For in that fair land, where the purified stand,
Our faith will be sight, and in its pure light,
We'll crave not the joys left behind.

Andante.

GENTLE DEEDS.

MT. LEBANON, N. Y.

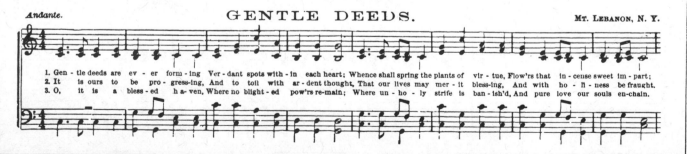

1. Gen - tle deeds are ev - er form - ing Ver-dant spots with-in each heart; Whence shall spring the plants of vir - tue, Flow'rs that in-cense sweet im - part;
2. It is ours to be pro-gress-ing, And to toil with ar-dent thought, That our lives may mer - it bless-ing, And with ho - li - ness be fraught.
3. O, it is a bless - ed ha - ven, Where no blight - ed pow'rs re-main; Where un-ho - ly strife is ban-ish'd, And pure love our souls en-chain.

GENTLE DEEDS—Continued.

Such shall wa - ken thoughts most ho - ly; Bring to life some germ of love; Cause as - pir - ings true and last - ing, For the powers that lift a - bove.
Morn shall o - pe with new de - sires; Eve-ning shall their strength increase; While the an - gels find our spir - its Rest-ing in the realms of peace.
Here in u - nion we are leav - ing All the glit' - ring dust of earth; Seek - ing on - ly the im - mor - tal, Which will give us an - gel birth.

FESTIVE SONG.

MT. LEBANON, N. Y.

1. Praise, rejoicing and thanks-giv - ing, Is the glo - ry of our song! While the an-gels from a - bove us, Waft the bles - sed strain a - long;
2. May the joy our feel - ings cherish, Thrill a chord in ev' - ry heart! While the secret streams out-flow - ing, Shall an an - swer true im-part;

'Tis for promised joys unmeasured, For delights that ne'er will wane, For the rapture pure be - fore us, And the hope for ho - ly gain.
And we call on all to join us In our joy-ous fes - tive song! While the waves of life dance mer - ry, And the heart is glad and strong!

Chorus. *con spirito.*

We will swell the gladsome chorus, Till bright hosts around us throng, And with harps of sweetest mu - sic, Join our u - ni - ver - sal song.
Yea we'll swell the gladsome chorus, Full, un - broken, rich and strong; Till it floats and floats a - round us, This our u - ni - ver - sal song.

TWILIGHT REFLECTION.

MT. LEBANON, N. Y.

1. When the soft shades of twilight drop over our way, Like curtains let down from on high, When life's busy scenes that have crowded the day,
2. O, this is the sea-son when calm, holy thought Like tide-waves our spirits o'er-flow, While truest of pictures our life-deeds have wrought,
3. Then oft let us pause mid the con-flict and strife, The coun-sel of wis-dom to heed, To ask for a fore-taste of heav-en-ly life,

Have pass'd with the light from the sky; Tis then that the spi-rit should rise and take flight, From tu-mult of earth and its care,
Re - flec - tion shall o - ver us throw, Till clear - ly por-trayed on the vi - sion with-in, Each mo-tive and ac-tion will be,
To sa - tis - fy im - mor-tal need; And when the deep sha-dows of time close around, When life's fair-est day-beams are past,

And seek sweet re - pose on the sha-dow-less height, Com - mu - nion with an - gels to share.
The glo - ry of good-ness, the dark - ness of sin, In joy or in sor - row we see.
May light from be - yond us our path - way sur - round, For ev - er and ev - er to last.

BEAUTIFUL SHORE.

Andante. *rit.*

1. Time's dark bil - lows and tempests may roar, Yet will I sing of that beau-ti-ful shore, Where the chill winter of life shall be o'er, Ne'er to return to the soul.
2. Glad - some the spring of that fair happy land, Blossom and fruitage in glo - ry ex-pand, While the soft breeze from its emerald strand, Scent-laden floats to us here.
3. Pil - grims who tar - ry, your time yet abide, Slowly re - ced - ing is life's eb-bing tide; O - ver its sur - ges your spi-rits shall glide Safe to that beau-ti - ful shore.

Blest summer land, free from sorrow and gloom, In fadeless beauty our spirits shall bloom, While the earth casket in-her - its the tomb, Sea-sons su - per-nal will roll.
Love builds its mansion all pearly and bright, Rising in grandeur in rose-tinted light; 'Tis for the blessed, whose robes are made white, Heavenly homes have been rear'd.
Hap - py the tho't! If our hearts are made pure, We an in - her - it-ance there shall secure. Hope still confides in the prom - is-es sure, When here our journey is o'er.

THE SILVER LINING.

CAANAN, N. Y.

1. Though dark clouds may often ga-ther That would make our pathway drear, An - gel voi - ces sweetly ut - ter Lo, the sil - ver lin-ing's near.
2. Hope and faith shall e'er sustain us, While for hea - ven we pre - pare, For be - yond the darkest sha-dow Lies a sil - ver lin - ing there.

Chorus.

O the glo-ri-ous sil-ver lin - ing, See the clouds now break a - way, In-spi - ra-tion's light is shin-ing, Ush-'ring in the heav'n-ly day.

PROGRESSION.

MT. LEBANON N. Y.

1. Be firm our en-dea-vor to fol-low the right, Though ma-ny our pur-pose op-pose,
2. The hill of re-demp-tion with cou-rage we'll climb, Though rug-ged our path-way and steep,
3. The dark-ness of doubt that be-cloud-ed our way, Fades far in the dis-tance from sight,

The weapons we wield are untarnish'd and bright, And mighty to vanquish our foes, We will join the vic-to-ri-ous ar-my of truth
Un-flinch-ing 'mid tri-als and dan-gers of time, Still sunward our course we will keep, For a sweet sound of triumph floats down from the spheres
We press for the glo-ry of e-ter-nal day, Where lingers no shadow or blight, We will swell the grand chorus with heaven's bright throng

Whose van-guard be-fore us have gone, They tra-verse the land of per-pe-tu-al youth, All crown'd with the lau-rels they've won.
There's joy in the con-quer-or's song, With hope all in-spir-ing with glad-ness it cheers, And hastens our jour-ney a-long.
The bless-ing of vic-to-ry see, The con-quest of self o-ver er-ror and wrong, The life that re-mains for the free.

PROMISE.

MT. LEBANON, N. Y.
Omit the Rest to the first verse.

1. We'll breathe the words of ho - ly joy, To spi - rits who are cast
2. We'll guide you to the glad - some sphere, Where pu - rest toils a - bound,
3. And you shall see we are not bound By self - ish - ness or pride,

Up - on the sor - row'd waves of life, Where bit - ter - ness doth last; We'll tell you of a hap - py home
And show to you the heaven-ly truth Our pil - grim - age hath found; We'll ope the se - cret of our joys,
But self - de - ni - al is the power In which our souls a - bide; That all we have is spent for God,

Be - yond the strife of care, Where love is reign-ing in each heart, And deeds are wrought in prayer.
The plea - sures of our day, And give you from our trea - su - ry, Till grief shall pass a - way.
To aid the fall - en race, And make this earth, on which we live, A par - a - dise of grace.

KEYS OF REVELATION.

MT. LEBANON, N. Y.

1. The type of life pro — gress - ive, Viewed by a seer of old,

To the en - light - ened vis - ion In mean - ing doth un - fold. As - cend - ing and de - scend - ing

The pure and shin - ing way, The mes - sen - gers of heav - en Re - vis - it earth to - day.

2.
They come, O earth! to bless thee,
Their loving mission hail!
They sow beside all waters
The seed that cannot fail,
Truth's precious germs upspringing
Shall fruit immortal bear,
Rich prophecy of blessing
Which many souls will share.

3.
The ministry of angels
Shall light the darkened land,
'Till earth's benighted children
God's power will understand ;
'Till Babel towers of error
To their foundations reel,
And gilded temple glories
A mighty shock will feel.

4.
The keys of Revelation,
Which long were doomed to rust,
Now ope the golden portals
Of saving faith and trust ;
The soul unfolds her pinions
To rise from nature's gloom,
For strength of resurrection
Lies not within her tomb.

PRAYER AND PRAISE.

(Sentiment taken from Fifth Psalm.)

MT. LEBANON, N. Y.

1. Un - to my words, O Lord, give ear, My me - di - ta - tion heed, While low - ly bow'd in sa - cred fear, Thy strength my soul doth need;
2. My voice, O God, in morn-ing light, I will di - rect in pray'r, Guide thou my wand'ring thoughts aright, And shield me by thy care;

O, hearken when to Thee I cry, Thou art my hope and stay, I feel Thy spi - rit draw-ing nigh, When un-to Thee I pray.
Though tempting snares my path be - set Stead-fast my faith shall be, Thy prom-ise I will not for - get, But look for help from Thee.

3.

In wickedness and vanity No pleasure dost Thou show,
No evil thing shall dwell with Thee, All wrong Thou wilt o'erthrow;
The false shall not stand in Thy sight, The flattering tongue thou't bind,
For truth with clear and glowing light Will search the heart and mind.

4.

Those who rebel against Thy law, And in defiance sin,
Upon their souls true judgment draw, And feel its pang within;
But as for me I'll seek a place Within God's house of prayer,
Where dwelleth mercy, truth and grace, My soul shall worship there.

5.

Within Thy temple songs of praise Shall evermore resound,
In anthems sweet my voice I'll raise For blessings that abound;
Let them rejoice that in Thee trust, And shout in songs of joy,
Thou ever wilt defend the just Who evil works destroy.

6.

Those who Thy name adore and love, Shall sound a joyful strain,
As they advance to realms above, Away from earth's low plane;
Thy favor to the righteous show, O Lord be thou their shield,
Till they Thy perfect life shall know, In endless light reveal'd.

EDEN OF TO-DAY.

MT. LEBANON, N. Y.

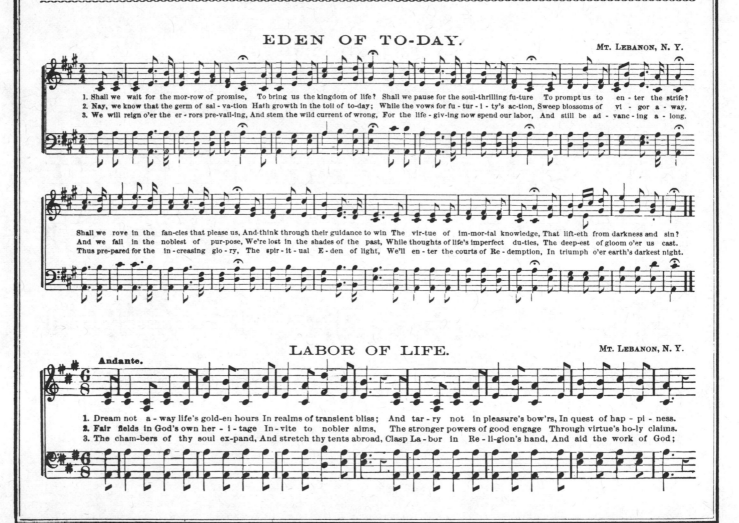

1. Shall we wait for the mor-row of promise, To bring us the kingdom of life? Shall we pause for the soul-thrilling fu-ture To prompt us to en - ter the strife?
2. Nay, we know that the germ of sal - va-tion Hath growth in the toil of to-day; While the vows for fu - tur - i - ty's ac-tion, Sweep blossoms of vi - gor a - way.
3. We will reign o'er the er - rors pre-vail-ing, And stem the wild current of wrong, For the life - giv-ing now spend our labor, And still be ad - vanc-ing a - long.

Shall we rove in the fan-cies that please us, And think through their guidance to win The vir-tue of im-mor-tal knowledge, That lift-eth from darkness and sin?
And we fail in the noblest of pur-pose, We're lost in the shades of the past, While thoughts of life's imperfect du-ties, The deep-est of gloom o'er us cast.
Thus pre-pared for the in-creasing glo-ry, The spir-it-ual E - den of light, We'll en - ter the courts of Re - demption, In triumph o'er earth's darkest night.

LABOR OF LIFE.

MT. LEBANON, N. Y.

Andante.

1. Dream not a - way life's gold-en hours In realms of transient bliss; And tar - ry not in pleasure's bow'rs, In quest of hap - pi - ness.
2. Fair fields in God's own her - i - tage In-vite to nobler aims, The stronger powers of good engage Through virtue's ho-ly claims.
3. The cham-bers of thy soul ex-pand, And stretch thy tents abroad, Clasp La - bor in Re - li-gion's hand, And aid the work of God;

LABOR OF LIFE—Continued.

For there the sy-ren sings her song, The wand-'rer to de-coy, There sub-tle charms like magnet strong, Allure but to de-stroy.
A-wake! for glorious themes to strive, Above earth's sordid pelf, In broad phi-lan-thro-phy to thrive, Beyond the sphere of self.
Till the mil-len-nial day shall shine Unto earth's distant bound; Till per-fect love, and peace di-vine, A - bi-ding place have found.

ETERNITY'S GAIN.

MT. LEBANON N. Y.

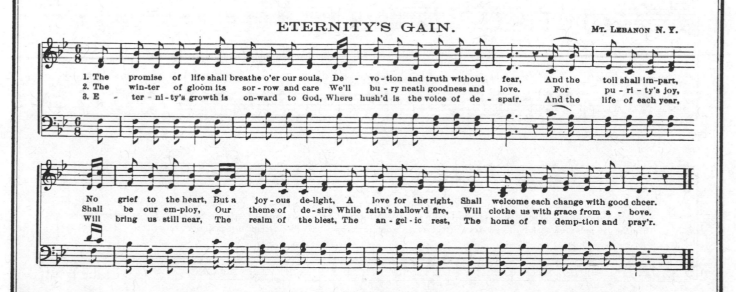

1. The promise of life shall breathe o'er our souls, De - vo-tion and truth without fear, And the toil shall im-part,
2. The win-ter of gloom its sor - row and care We'll bu - ry neath goodness and love. For pu - ri - ty's joy,
3. E - ter - ni-ty's growth is on-ward to God, Where hush'd is the voice of de - spair. And the life of each year,

No grief to the heart, But a joy - ous de-light, A love for the right, Shall welcome each change with good cheer.
Shall be our em-ploy, Our theme of de - sire While faith's hallow'd fire, Will clothe us with grace from a - bove.
Will bring us still near, The realm of the blest, The an - gel - ic rest, The home of re demp-tion and pray'r.

CALL TO THE WEARY.

Mt. Lebanon, N. Y.

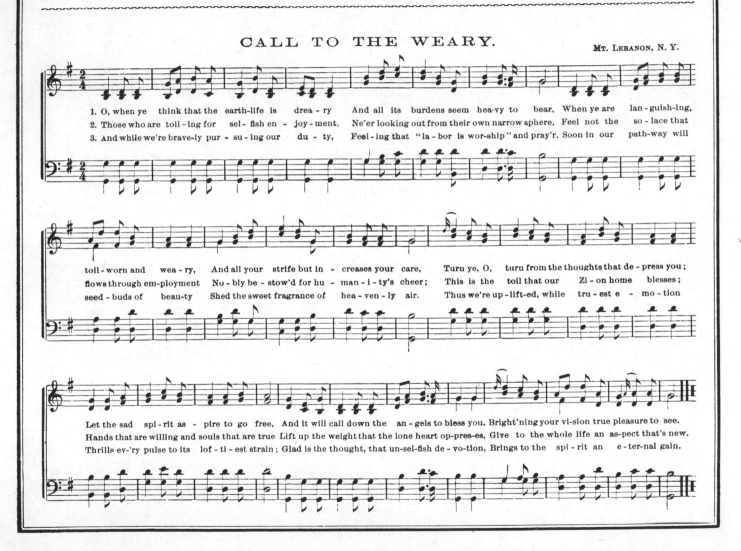

1. O, when ye think that the earth-life is drea - ry And all its burdens seem hea-vy to bear, When ye are lan - guish-ing,
2. Those who are toil - ing for sel - fish en - joy-ment, Ne'er looking out from their own narrow sphere, Feel not the so - lace that
3. And while we're brave-ly pur - su - ing our du - ty, Feel - ing that "la - bor is wor-ship" and pray'r, Soon in our path-way will

toil - worn and wea - ry, And all your strife but in - creases your care, Turn ye, O, turn from the thoughts that de - press you;
flows through em-ployment No - bly be - stow'd for hu - man - i - ty's cheer; This is the toil that our Zi - on home blesses;
seed - buds of beau - ty Shed the sweet fragrance of hea - ven - ly air. Thus we're up - lift-ed, while tru - est e - mo - tion

Let the sad spi - rit as - pire to go free, And it will call down the an - gels to bless you, Bright'ning your vi-sion true pleasure to see.
Hands that are willing and souls that are true Lift up the weight that the lone heart op-pres-es, Give to the whole life an as-pect that's new.
Thrills ev-'ry pulse to its lof - ti - est strain; Glad is the thought, that un-sel-fish de - vo-tion, Brings to the spi - rit an e - ter-nal gain.

BEAUTIFUL ANGEL HOME.

MT. LEBANON N. Y.

1. O, my beau - ti - ful an-gel home! Fraught with blessing and peace, Where no sor-row of earth can come, Where in - har - mo-nies cease;

2. Storm and tempest may wildly reign, Clouds as dark as the night, Gath-er o - ver the gold-en plain, Shutting thy glo-ry from sight.

Bas'd and built on the rock of truth, Rear'd by an Al - mighty arm, Heav'n-ly vi-gils pro-tect thy youth, From all dan-ger and harm.

Shall not hands of a ho - ly pow'r, Chase and scat-ter the mist, That the light of a bright-er hour, With thee may ev-er ex - ist?

Chorus.

O, my beau-ti - ful an-gel home! Fraught with blessing and peace, Bright immortals around thee come, Crowning with joy thy in - crease.

3.

Thus the care of a father kind, And a mother's pure love,
Bid thee prosper and union find To fair Zion above;
Storm, and tempest and cloud defied, God thy life and support,
Hosts of heaven upon thy side, Light to the nations thou art.
CHORUS: O, my beautiful, etc.

4.

Bound to hearts that are willing here, Toil and labor are mine,
Till my spirit and life appear In thy glory to shine;
Till thy truth like a flood shall roll, O'er a sin-darkened earth,
Drawing hither the burdened soul, Weary of spiritual dearth.
CHORUS: O, my beautiful, etc.

BEAUTIFUL VALLEY.

MT. LEBANON N. Y.

1. I am seek-ing a beau-ti-ful val-ley, Its path-way I ne'er before knew, And as I am slow-ly de-scend-ing, Its beau-ties un-fold to my view;
2. 'Tis true the de-scent has been painful, With watching, and toil and great care, I've been prosper'd thus far on my journey, And now grow content with my fare;
3. There are pilgrims descending be-fore me, They all have some good thing to say Of hu-mil-i-ty's beau-ti-ful val-ley, And al-so of Zi-on's high-way;

A-way in my old na-tive ci-ty, I dream'd of this land far a-way, But thought it a de-so-late re-gion, And dreaded the rough thorny way.
I find that each step I have ta-ken, But gives new ex-pe-ri-ence and strength, My courage is strong and un-sha-ken, I'll gain the blest valley at length.
For just through the midst of the lowland, Is a high-way of ho-li-ness clean, The li-on this path hath not trod-den, Nor eye of the vul-ture e'er seen.

OUR MISSION.

CANAAN, N. Y.

1. We all have a du-ty of life to per-form, A mis-sion of love to ful-fill;

OUR MISSION—Continued.

A work that is wor - thy our pow'rs to en - gage, With firm - ness of pur - pose and will.

We all have a jour - ney of life to pur - sue, The high - way of pro - gress to climb;

A strife to en - dure, and a vic - t'ry to win, 'Mid per - ils and dan - gers of time.

2.
And should we not linger to proffer our aid,
  To those who with trials oppress'd,
Are leaving the earthly for treasures divine,
  Who're seeking but finding no rest?
And shall we not give all our feelings in prayer,
  For souls who are yearning for light,
And place in the pathway of safety and truth
  The upward bound traveler aright?

3.
O, yea! we can brighten with smiles of good cheer,
  The way of the downcast and sad,
And give to the sin-sick a promise of hope,
  The sorrowing spirit make glad.
We can comfort the mourner with tidings of joy,
  And lighten life's burden and care;
Uplifting the spirits of those who are bound,
  The blessings of freedom to share.

4.
We can hush the wild tumult of discord and strife
  With love's gentle accents of peace,
And welcome the weary worn pilgrim to rest,
  Where storms of contention shall cease.
O, this is our mission, and this is our call,
  To resurrect souls from the earth,
And aid them, through high aspiration, to rise,
  To joys of the angelic birth.

HOME OF PEACE.

CANAAN, N. Y.

Home, home, home! There's beauty rife on every side, At golden morn and even-tide; Home, sweet home! And music in the tran-quil air, That

floats a - round thy   bor - ders fair, Home, sweet home! The world has lost its charms for me, For pur - er joy I   find in thee,

O, home, sweet home! Joy which the world can never know, In thee from sac-red   love doth flow, O, home, sweet home!   A holy peace un-

marred by sin, Is grav-en on thy walls within ; And sacred or-ders guard thee round, And safely shield on hallowed ground, Home, sweet home !

THE GLAD NEW YEAR!

Mt. Lebanon, N. Y.

1. A-'long the sha-dowy aisles of time, there floats a murmur soft and low, Now swell-ing in har-mo-nious chime,

sweet notes in mea-sured numbers flow. With joy we catch the glad-some strain, which fills our hearts with lov-ing cheer,

And, echo-ing back a true re-frain, give wel-come to the Glad New Year!

2. Our hopes on starry pinions rise, High aspiration thrills our soul,
A nobler life to realize, Ascending to perfection's goal,
The past with joy and sorrow fraught, Shall from our vision disappear;
The present claims our earnest thought: All hail the bright, the Glad New Year!

3. Like angels from the realms unseen, Light-wing'd the moments come and go,
The shining links of life, between Ethereal spheres and earth below;
They bear a record of the deeds That cloud, or make our pathway clear:
Broadcast they sow time's precious seeds, And usher in the Glad New Year!

4. We tread the vale of time and sense, Amid its phantom-fleeting dreams,
Still longing, with a hope intense, For something that enduring seems;
Yet duty's path we will pursue, Without a doubt or cringing fear;
With lofty aim and purpose true, We'll toil throughout the Glad New Year;

5. The tender chords of purest love, With peace entwined, shall stronger grow!
We'll bear the spirit of the dove, And kindness to the erring show;
With gentle words, and Christ-like deeds, A monument of good we'll rear;
While bliss, that fills our spirit needs, Awaits us in the Glad New Year!

LAND OF LOVE.

MT. LEBANON, N. Y.

1. Veil not from us Ho-ly Spi-rit, Beau-ties that are ev-er rife, In our fu-ture home of glo-ry, Land of love and end-less life.

Lift the cur-tain from our vi-sion, Fan the mists that dim our eyes; We would scan the in-ner hea-vens And from earth-li-ness a-rise.

2. We would take the wings of morning,
   And explore the mountain's height;
Or descend in pleasant valleys,
   Seeking treasures free from blight;
In a blessed sweet communion
   With the loved ones gone before,
We would clasp them nearer to us,
   Range with them the heavenly shore.

3. But we'll bide our time in patience,
   And improve each moment well,
In a life of consecration
   We will labor to excel.
Forming here a joyous heaven,
   By creating one within;
And a home of love and beauty,
   Free from discord, strife and sin.

4. Then abide, O blessed spirit!
   Purify us unto thee,
That a tower of strength and glory
   To the nations we may be ;
And our earthly home foreshadow
   Our eternal home above ;
Dwelling place of truth and goodness,
   Paradise of heavenly love.

RETIREMENT.

CANAAN, N. Y.

Dolce.

1. When a-lone and re-tir'd in the soul's si-lent cham-ber, With thoughts fix'd on heav-en-ly treasures a-bove,
2. 'Tis a time when the soul while in deep-est e-mo-tion, Can new-ly as-pire for the unc-tion of Christ,

RETIREMENT—Continued.

The an-gels endow'd with the true resurrection, Waft to our spirits the balm of sweet love. How cheering the thought, that a time for reflection
Can press for the blessing, in fer-vent de-vo-tion, Un-fold-ing growth, of the an-gel-ic life. Tis a sea-son of peaceful, and ho-ly se-clu-sion.

Will ban-ish all sorrow and fear from the heart, Will brighten the hopes of the future before us, And un-to our spir-its sweet solace impart.
When we for the life that's e-ter-nal prepare, Remote from the world with its strife and confusion, Blest hour of retirement, I'll spend thee in pray'r

TRIUMPH.

MT. LEBANON, N. Y.

For the triumph o'er self, and the reign of free-dom, We are toi-ling in spi-rit day un-to day; Our re-ward and honor are

ev-er with us, As we joy-ous-ly march the life-giving way. And yet we are yearn-ing for a fur-ther glory, When

faith—though pu-ri-ty—is changed to sight; And our eyes be-hold the im-mor-tal rich-es, That are trea-sured for us in the land of light.

WELCOME.

MT. LEBANON, N. Y.

When the first soft flush of morn-ing Stole o'er the eas-tern sky, And the stars' last gleams were fading From yon blue vault on high;
Now we hear the glad-some voi-ces From na-ture's vast do-main; They have caught the welcome cho-rus, And e-cho back the strain,

The earth was robed in beau - ty, Yet fair - er than its grace, Ap-pear'd to us the dear ones Whose presence bless this place.
The trees with mu - sic trem-ble, The sunbeam glances tell Of the un - cloud-ed plea-sure That reigns where an-gels dwell.

Chorus.

O, wel-come! wel-come to our feast! On this fair hal-low'd ground, From ev' - ry heart re-spond-ing, Sweet wel-come echoes round.
O, wel-come! wel-come we re-peat, To call your bless-ing down, Your lov-ing presence with us, Our feast with joy shall crown.

TIMES OF REFRESHING.

MT. LEBANON, N. Y.

The Spi - rit and Bride are call-ing come! Let all who hear re - echo the sound! The Lord has pre - pared for His

peo - ple at home, Where the power of sal - va-tion is found. O joy - ful the tid-ings! the an - gels are glad, That the times of re -

fresh-ing have come; And the du - al voice of Christ now is heard, Gent - ly call - ing the sin - sick and wea-ry home.

JOURNEYING ON.

Mt. Lebanon, N. Y.

1. Our faith is un-cloud-ed and bright as the day, Up-lift-ing our spir-its from dark-ness a-way;
2. The high-way of ho-li-ness we will pur-sue, While plea-sures ter-res-trial re-cede from our view;
3. Brave pil-grims who tra-versed this way in the past, With pure hal-low'd bless-ings our spir-its o'er-cast;
4. Though thorny the path-way a-wait-ing our feet, And ma-ny the dan-gers and tri-als we meet,

No sha-dow of turn-ing our pro-gress shall stay, We're bound for the re-gions of bliss.
We'll sip from the foun-tain of life that is new, And feast on the fruits of pure love.
They scat-ter'd the seed-germs of truth that will last, In beau-ty for-ev-er to bloom.
With cou-rage un-daunt-ed no power can de-feat, We'll press for the heav-en-ly goal.

Chorus. *spirited.* p *full*

We are jour-ney-ing on, we are jour-ney-ing on, To the love land of light, our beau-ti-ful home!

Where sin can-not blight nor sor-row e'er come, O, beau-ti-ful, blest and e-ter-nal home.

STAR OF HOPE.

MT. LEBANON, N. Y.

Bright - ly beam - eth the star of hope on my way, I will fol - low the light of its cheer - ing ray; Blest

o - men of peace, shine on to the day— When hap - pi - ness ne'er shall fail. No gloom shall a - rise like the dark - ness of night to ob-

scure the gleam of thy ho - ly light; By thy guid - ance my soul shall take its flight, Be - yond earth's shadowy vale.

CITY OF LIGHT.

Andante.

CANAAN SOUTH FAMILY.

1. There o - pen be - fore me, in vi - sions of glo - ry, Bright scenes of that fair sum - mer land,
2. When the rude storms of life and its tem - pests have end - ed, Sweet prai - ses our hearts shall em - ploy,

Where, in beau - ty and gran - deur, God's Ci - ty of Light A bea - con for - ev - er will stand;
Where the soft, bal - my zephyrs of soul - cheer - ing love Bring glad - ness re - plete with true joy.

CITY OF LIGHT—Continued.

There, pure crys-tal foun-tains for-ev-er are flow-ing, Whose riv-ers make glad the op-press'd,
In vi-sion I see thee, thou beau-ti-ful Ci-ty! There's nothing so love-ly be-low;

And mu-sic su-per-nal breathes tid-ings of peace, To wel-come the pil-grim to rest.
And, when I've re-lin-quish'd the ties of this earth, To thy bliss-ful man-sions I'll go.

TIME IS PASSING.

SOUTH UNION, KY.

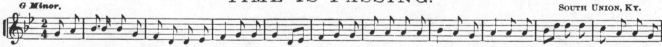

O, how swiftly time is passing, and 'tis precious to me, My moments are roll-ing as the waves of the sea, They are solemn and weighty as they

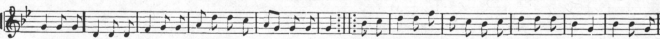

roll one by one, And ex-claim with a meaning ev-er gone, ev-er gone! But, a-las! for its pleasures, they are vain! they are gay! they perish with

us-ing and soon pass a-way! And time, time is call-ing ev'-ry mo-ment to me, A-rise and be liv-ing for e-ter-ni-ty.

HEAVENLY PROSPECT.

ENFIELD, N. H.

Oh, the pros-pect be - fore me, what a theme for thought ! What con-vul-sions of nature and con - ver-sions of heart ! What

fields to be traversed, how ex - tensive how grand ! Be - fore our spi - rits with an-gels can blend. I am on my

jour-ney to that beau - ti - ful land, I am on my journey to that beau - ti - ful land Where the an - gels dwell, where the

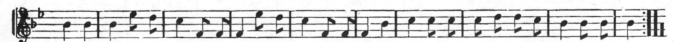

an-gels dwell ; To that bright spi-rit land so en - tranc - ing to mind, The home of my Parents, there I'm bound, I am bound !

LET ZION MOVE!

ALFRED, ME.

Let Zi-on move as the heart of one, Her light shine forth as the rising sun, And let her people all become bap - tized with fire from heaven

Send ho-ly in - spir - a-tion down, Hea-ven - ly Fa - ther, from Thy throne ; Leave, O leave us not a - lone ! Angel guides di - rect us.

MORNING LIGHT.

Mt. Lebanon, N. Y.

1. The res-ur-rec-tion an - gels call, a - wak - en is the cry! The East is filled with morning light; the clouds of darkness fly!
2. 'Tis not a time of hope-less grief, though truth's un-fail-ing fire— Con-sumes the earthly elements, and every vain de - sire;
3. And when the burn-ing time is o'er, O, who will count its pain! A - mid the glo-ries and the love, that ne'er shall fade a - gain.

This is the day of righteousness; for now hath Christ appeared! Be - hold, up-on the mountain height, his snowy banner reared!
The sea of thought gives up its dead, and naught will memory hide; But by this judgment of the Lord, the soul is pu - ri - fied.
With strength I will sustain my part, and press through every ill, Un - til I reach that blest abode, the City on the hill.

NEW YEAR'S GREETING.

Mt. Lebanon, N. Y.

1. Listen! while we join with an-gels, Who in love have gathered near; And we'll tell you of the morning—Of the glorious day that's dawning—Of the new and coming year.

2.
Clean shall be our future pages,
  Stamped upon our memory clear;
Free from sin, and void of sadness --
Fraught with joy and full of gladness -
Record of the coming year.

3.
And we'll touch the muse, to waken—
  Those who are to us so dear;
Wishing all a happy morning,
Happy weeks and months are dawning,
  And withal a happy year.

WILLING SACRIFICE.

MT. LEBANON, N. Y.

1. What is in thy heart for God? search its depths and see, If thou hast a place for Him, kept in pu - ri - ty.
2. What is in thy heart for God? are thy joys of earth? Or, hast thou deep hap - pi - ness, of en - dur-ing worth?

Mid the treasures of thy life — treasures with - out price — Hast thou ev - er for the Lord, a will-ing sac - ri - fice?
And art thou a fruit - ful branch, of the liv - ing tree, Clothed with innocence, with peace, and true hu-mil - i - ty?

3.

What is in thy heart for God?
  Do thy hopes ascend
Unto truth and holiness
  That shall never end?
Is thy love a living fount —
  Gushing, bright and clear?
Doth the image of the Lord
  Within its source appear?

4.

All I have, I give to God
  And His blessed cause!
Praying, that my life may be
  Guided by His laws.
Lead me, Holy Spirit, down
  Till I see my loss!
Strengthen me to do the work
  That cometh by the cross.

BLESSINGS.

MT. LEBANON, N. Y.

O Parents we thank you for all the blest powers, Which bring in their season, the sun-shine and showers;

Sweet dews and soft breez - es, the shadows and light, The glo - ry of day and the si - lence of night.

O bless the fair vint-age, the orchard and field, That fruit in a - bund-ance to us they may yield;

And here in our home which bless-ings have crowned, We'll toil in one spi - rit that good may a - bound.

BRIGHT GUIDING STARS.

ALFRED, ME.

Oh, bright shining an - gels and spi - rits of the just, Made perfect through suf - fer-ing, our hope and trust; Ye are

our guid-ing stars through the jour-ney of life,— Our com-fort and sweet con-sol - a - tion. All hail ye mes-sen-gers of

truth and love! Ye bring to us tid-ings from the city a - bove; Ye tell us of the glo - ries of that far bet - ter clime,

Where our bright guiding stars .... e - ter - nal - ly shine — Our bright guid-ing stars e - ter - nal - ly shine.

HOME.

MT. LEBANON, N. Y.

m

1. We have a home from the cold world hid, A spot con - se - cra-ted to God; And our feet are shod for the blest high-way
2. Here we can ban - ish the cares of earth, And fan-cies that lead a - stray; 'Tis here we strive that the an - gel death
3. Here waves of love a - round us roll, And o - pen the beau-ties of grace; Till their pow - er of good be - comes for us

H O M E—Continued.

Which the ran-som'd be-fore have trod. Here the star of In - no - cence for - ev - er shines; And beams of Char - 1 - ty glow;
May nev - er be-cloud our way. Thus the growth of a life in God is ours, The strength of the Con-quer-or's light,
A heav - en - ly home and place. And thus we're hid from a cold world's gaze, To know of a sin - less rest;

Here the in-ner thoughts are attuned through faith, To vir-tue's me - lo - di - ous flow, To vir-tue's me - lo - di - ous flow.
The joy that fu - tu - ri-ty's bliss re-veals, With im - mor - tal - i - ty bright, With im - mor - tal - i - ty bright.
When the breath of our being up-ward wings, To float in the land of the blest, To float in the land of the blest.

Chorus. *mp*

O home for the soul, Heaven be-gun be - low; We'll sing of thy beau-ty and tell of thy joys, Till all thy glo - ry shall know.

HUNDRED-FOLD BLESSING.

MT. LEBANON, N. Y.

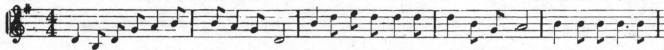

Give me the treasure that can-not be sold; Give me that Gos-pel that wax-eth not old; Give me that love which

will not grow cold, And I am blest with a hundred-fold. Then will the shadows of er-ror's dark night—Flee, flee be-

fore the morn-ing light; Then will that faith ex - ceed-ing-ly bright, Shine,. . shine o'er my path in the right.

THE COMING YEAR.

Joyous.

MT. LEBANON, N. Y.

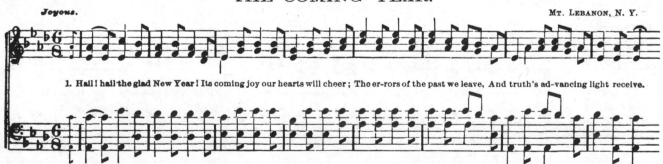

1. Hail! hail the glad New Year! Its coming joy our hearts will cheer; The er-rors of the past we leave, And truth's ad-vancing light receive.

THE COMING YEAR—Continued.

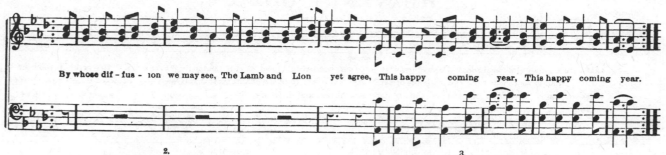

By whose dif-fus-ion we may see, The Lamb and Lion yet agree, This happy coming year, This happy coming year.

2.
Though labors new await our hands,
We will not bind in iron bands
The talent God to us hath given
To make our home on earth a heav'n.
But sow anew the precious grain,
And scatter broadcast o'er the plain,
This joyous coming year,
This joyous coming year.

3.
The seeds of goodness, love and peace,
Of kindness with its rich increase,
These in our hearts' best soil shall live,
Till blossoms sweet their perfume give,
While ripen'd grain in sheaves well bound,
Shall in our garner-room be found,
This joyous happy year,
This joyous happy year.

ANGEL'S SONG.

UNION VILLAGE, OHIO.

I hear the sweet sound of an an-gel song, From regions a-way in the hea-vens! With mus-ic su-per-nal it

trem-bles a-long, Re-fresh-ing the land of the liv-ing. I feel the en-chant-ment of hea-ven-ly love, Now

wav-ing de-light-ful-ly o'er me; Ser-ene-ly dis-till-ing from spi-rits above, Who've journeyed to hea-ven be-fore me.

HEAVENLY GOAL.

CANAAN, N. Y.

1. We are all marching on through the shadows of time To our beau-ti-ful, beau-ti-ful home! Where a - mid the green bowers of
2. Oh,   glad-ly we're leav - ing the lowlands of earth, Where we dwelt 'mid the phantoms that perished; Where the pro-mise of pleasure but
3. We've tasted the bliss of the hea-ven-ly state, And have found the rich pearl of sal-va-tion; The   pure in-spi-ra-tion of

Wisdom and Love, In the sun-shine of truth we will roam;   We'll sing of the bless - ings of life that a-bound For the
end-ed in pain, And vain were the hopes that we cherished;   Oh, cheer-ing the thought! we've o - beyed the high call, And have
e - ter-nal truth, Is the joy of our vir-gin re - la-tion;   Then up - ward through tri - al our watch-word will be, In the

up-right, the faithful and ho-ly; And ga-ther the flow-ers of vir - tue and peace, As we tra-vel to regions of glory.
en-tered the sphere of progression; We'll toil for the treas-ure of im - mor-tal worth, Our on - ly a-bid-ing pos-ses-sion.
light that is ev - er in-creas-ing; Re-demption's the goal we're de - ter - mined to win, For this will our strife be un-ceas-ing.

TRUE LOVE.

UNION VILLAGE, O.

1. Purer than the skies of even, Brighter than the morn-ing sun, Is that angel love from heaven, Blending all our hearts in one.

Now like rip'pling wa - ters meeting; Murmuring gladness to our ears, Now with-in our hearts tis beating, Mar - ches to the brighter spheres.

2. Oh, it is a glorious feeling, deep'ning as we heavenward go,
Spotless as the sunlight, stealing softly through the falling snow;
'Tis a fount of living waters, with rich blessings running o'er,
Where all Zion's sons and daughters, drink of bliss and thirst no more.

3. Love will heal the broken hearted, it will cure the stricken soul;
'Twill unite whom death has parted, where no waves of sorrow roll.
It will triumph when the mountains, time, at last, shall overthrow,
And when silent, all life's fountains, love shall bright, still brighter glow.

4. Like the light of hope that's beaming, o'er the dark clouds rolling high,
Love reveals far o'er them gleaming, brighter worlds beyond the sky.
Grant, thou Great Almighty Giver, o'er our wild and bleak domain,
Love may, like lost Eden's river, make this world to bloom again.

5. 'Tis to God and to each other, love unites us heart and hand,
And will guide us, sister, brother, homeward to the promised land;
While we pray to be forgiven, while we hope for heaven above,
May our strife be all for union, and our contest all for love.

PILGRIM BAND.

CANTERBURY, N. H.

Number me with the pil-grim band, Who're trav'ling to the promised land—Giv-ing to God both heart and hand—U - ni - ted for the truth to stand.

'Tis an up-hill work we're called un - to, An up-hill march till we've traveled through; Yet falter not be - loved few; For your re-ward is just and true.

COME TO ZION.

E Minor.   WATERVLEIT, N. Y.

Come to Zi - on, come to Zi - on, Sin - sick souls in sor - row bound! Lay your cares up - on the al - tar,

Where true heal-ing may be found. Shout Al - le - lu - ia! Al - le - lu - ia! Praise re-sounds o'er

land and sea; All who will may come and share The glo - ries of this Ju - bi - lee.

PILLAR OF LIGHT.

MT. LEBANON, N. Y.

A pil - lar of light is moving be-fore us, A cloud of witnesses leading us on To the fair land of promise—the new Jer-u - sa-lem;

With faith in our God we are valiant and strong, We'll move on, we'll go up and pos-sess the city—We'll march though her streets with our

banners unfurled; And the song of thanks-giving to God we are sounding, Who gathered us out from a lost sin-ful world.

MORNING DAWN.

MT. LEBANON, N. Y.

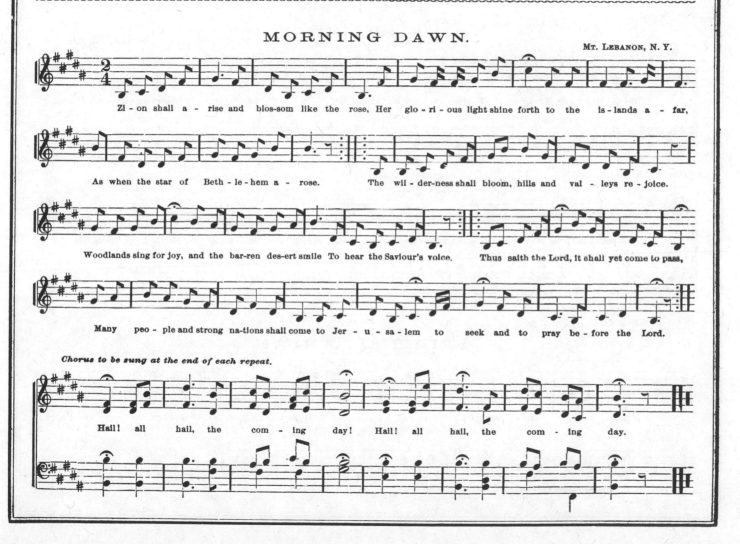

ONE SPARROW.

MT. LEBANON, N. Y.

Not one sparrow is for-got-ten,   E'en the   raven God will feed; And the   li - ly of the   val - ley,   Heaven grants its ev'-ry need.

Then shall I not trust thee, Father?   In thy   mercy have a share; And through faith and prayer, my Mother? Merit   thy protecting care?

SPIRIT OF TRUTH.

MT. LEBANON, N. Y.

Hail!   all   hail   thou im - mor-tal   Spi - rit of   Truth, Thy im-press is   stamped on the years! Though the

robes thou hast worn, have been blemished and torn, Still   glo - ri - ous thy presence ap - pears.   All   honor   to those who have

SPIRIT OF TRUTH—Continued.

stood for thy cause, And brave-ly have bat-tled their way— Through the dark storm and flood, still have cherished the good, That re-

mains to en-rich us to - day.   Then bless us for - ev- er,   O beau-ti - ful Spi-rit! May thy in-spi - ra-tion ne'er

fail — Our souls to sus-tain, till the vic-to - ry we gain, In thy strength we will sure-ly pre - vail.

"THE LORD REIGNETH."

UNION VILLAGE, OHIO.

The Lord in His ma-jes-ty reigneth supreme, O'er Zi - on the mount of sal - va - tion; O trust in His mer-cy, for

He will re-deem His chosen, from all tri-bu - la-tion.   What though He may lead us through dan-ger-ous ways, And

draped with the cur-tains of sor - row? This seem-ing af -flic-tion, and grief of to - day, May prove but His mer-cy to - mor-row

BLEST ZION.

WEST GLOUCESTER, ME.

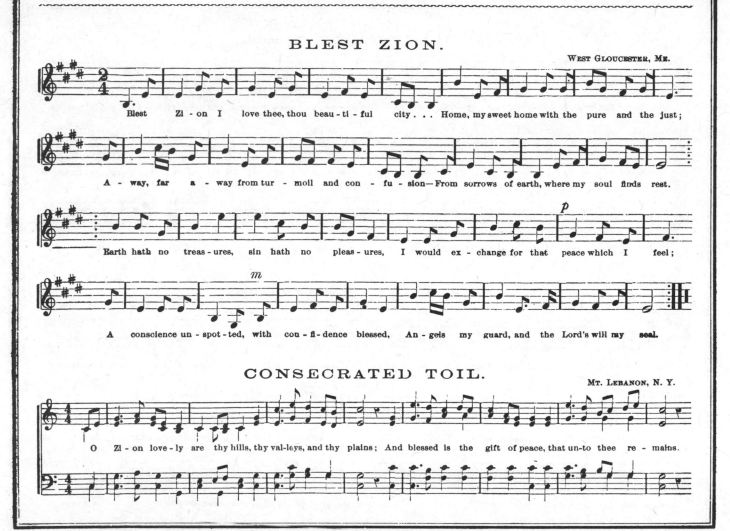

Blest Zi - on I love thee, thou beau - ti - ful city . . . Home, my sweet home with the pure and the just;

A - way, far a - way from tur - moil and con - fu - sion—From sorrows of earth, where my soul finds rest.

Earth hath no treas - ures, sin hath no pleas - ures, I would ex - change for that peace which I feel;

A conscience un - spot - ted, with con - fi - dence blessed, An - gels my guard, and the Lord's will my seal.

CONSECRATED TOIL.

MT. LEBANON, N. Y.

O Zi - on love - ly are thy hills, thy val - leys, and thy plains; And blessed is the gift of peace, that un - to thee re - mains.

CONSECRATED TOIL—Continued.

Our hearts are filled with joy and hope, in seed and blossom time ; For beauties like the heavenly worlds, have vis-i-ted our clime.

With thankfulness we come to God, u-ni-ted in a band, That he may bless our un-ion, our la-bor and our land.

Not for ourselves a-lone, we seek a harvest to se-cure ; We toil that we, with liberal hand, may feed the needy poor.

Remembering, that our parents toiled our birthright to se-cure— Remembering that our pa-rents toiled our birthright to se-cure.

FAREWELL.

MT. LEBANON, N. Y.

Fare - well, fare - well good friends in the cause ; Farewell till we meet once more ! If not here, In time in a fair sunny clime,

p Duet.   Cho.   *m* Duet.

We shall meet on the gold-en shore.   Shall peace be ev - er ours ? Sweet peace shall be ours.   Mid   hea - ven - ly flowers?

full Cho.   1ST.   2D.

Mid   hea-ven-ly flowers, That are scat-tered a - round us from an - gels a-bove, While winging their way on a mis-sion of   love.

FAREWELL—Continued.

Ho!.... Ho!.. Let us gather from heaven These gifts as they're given, And as the heart of one, Be u - ni - ted for - ev - er.

PURE LOVE.

MT. LEBANON, N. Y.

Pure love from the heaven of heavens de-scends Like show - ers up - on us to - day; And the an - gels of light, from their

realms so bright, Strew flow-ers all a - long our way. And the an - gel - ic choir, touch the strings of their lyre, And bid us with

cour-age move on; To en - ter the field, that so rich - ly will yield, A har - vest, when the victo - ry is won.

ANGELS' CALL.

MT. LEBANON, N. Y.

As an ar-my with ban-ners we are march-ing on, And we must not tar-ry by the way, For an-gels are call-ing,

call-ing us to come, And we will not tar-ry by the way. The pleasures of earth and its friendships we leave,

For we can-not tar-ry by the way, We are marching on our re-ward to re-ceive, And we will not tar-ry by the way.

CHRISTMAS MORN.

Mt. Lebanon, N. Y.

Hark! Hark, while we chant the sweet strain, Which once was heard on Judea's plain, When angels ushered in the reign, Of the low-ly Prince of peace.

"Good-will to man, and peace on earth," They sounded at our Sav-iour's birth, Their blessed song of joy and mirth, We will sound with an in-crease.

Peace! peace to all this Christmas morn, A-rise, for lo! the day doth dawn, Let Christian love and kind good will, Our hearts in-spire, our spi-rits fill.

COMING DAY.

MT. LEBANON, N. Y.

Heaven-ly joy il - lumes my way, Sweet peace o'er - shadows my path; And in the light of the com - ing day,

Off'rings of praise my spi - rit puts forth. For I be-hold the des - ert in blos - som, And the wil - der - ness

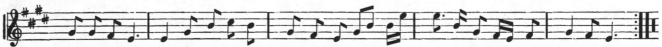

teem - ing with fruit; Ransomed souls are re - turn - ing to Zi - on, Filled with the ev - er - last - ing truth.

POWER OF LOVE.

MT. LEBANON, N. Y.

Afetuoso.

1. Sweet and mel - o - dious are the sounds I hear, Like an - gel mus - ic fall - ing on mine ear — From worlds a - bove·
2. This mighty pow - er the old heavens will shake, The earth will reel, and slumb'ring souls a - wake And cry to God!

POWER OF LOVE—Continued.

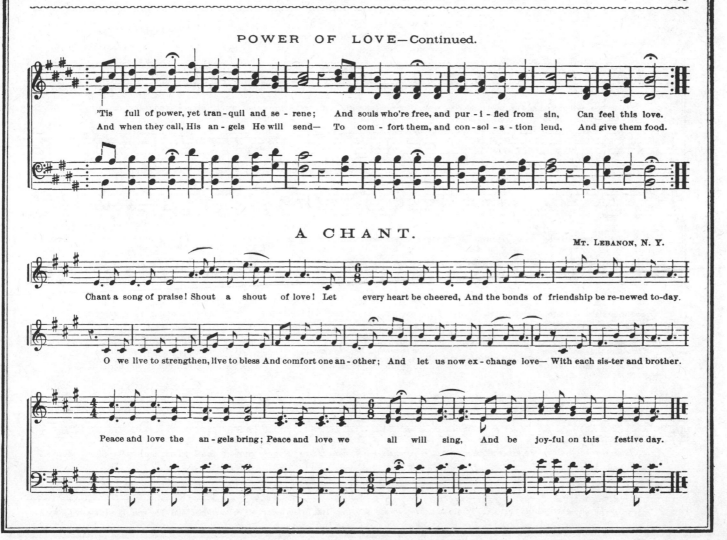

'Tis full of power, yet tran-quil and se - rene; And souls who're free, and pur-i-fied from sin, Can feel this love.

And when they call, His an-gels He will send— To com-fort them, and con-sol-a-tion lend, And give them food.

A CHANT.

Mt. Lebanon, N. Y.

Chant a song of praise! Shout a shout of love! Let every heart be cheered, And the bonds of friendship be re-newed to-day.

O we live to strengthen, live to bless And comfort one an-other; And let us now ex-change love— With each sis-ter and brother.

Peace and love the an-gels bring; Peace and love we all will sing, And be joy-ful on this festive day.

VOICE OF PEACE.

Mt. Lebanon, N. Y.

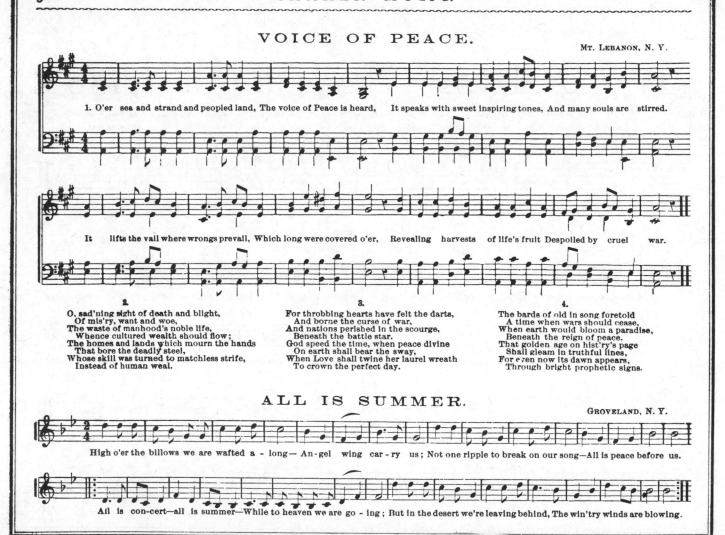

1. O'er sea and strand and peopled land, The voice of Peace is heard, It speaks with sweet inspiring tones, And many souls are stirred.

It lifts the vail where wrongs prevail, Which long were covered o'er, Revealing harvests of life's fruit Despoiled by cruel war.

2.
O, sad'ning sight of death and blight,
Of mis'ry, want and woe,
The waste of manhood's noble life,
Whence cultured wealth should flow;
The homes and lands which mourn the hands
That bore the deadly steel,
Whose skill was turned to matchless strife,
Instead of human weal.

3.
For throbbing hearts have felt the darts,
And borne the curse of war,
And nations perished in the scourge,
Beneath the battle star.
God speed the time, when peace divine
On earth shall bear the sway,
When Love shall twine her laurel wreath
To crown the perfect day.

4.
The bards of old in song foretold
A time when wars should cease,
When earth would bloom a paradise,
Beneath the reign of peace.
That golden age on hist'ry's page
Shall gleam in truthful lines,
For even now its dawn appears,
Through bright prophetic signs.

ALL IS SUMMER.

Groveland, N. Y.

High o'er the billows we are wafted a-long—An-gel wing car-ry us; Not one ripple to break on our song—All is peace before us.

All is con-cert—all is summer—While to heaven we are go-ing; But in the desert we're leaving behind, The win'try winds are blowing.

MESSENGER.

Mt. Lebanon, N. Y.

Go forth with the torch-lights, il-lumine the caves, The earth-ly con - di-tions that cov - er the soul; For morn-ing is shin-ing on

Jor-dan's deep waves, Call hither the wanderer to wash and be whole. O seek ye the sorrowful! seek ye the poor! And

show them the beau-ti-ful way of our Lord; O teach them the life that will ev - er endure, And God will your efforts re - ward.

TRIBUTE TO FRIENDS.

Mt. Lebanon, N. Y.

Oh, what can equal Gos - pel love, Which from a vir - gin life, Flows forth to meet its kindred tide, From

those who've won the strife. We do not ask for love and strength, But these we would im - part To those, who free-ly

have be-stow-ed, Upon the wea - ry heart. So we'll roll our song rich and strong, Up to the hea - ven - ly arches,

TRIBUTE TO FRIENDS—Continued.

And you shall catch the echoes long, From an - gels on their marches— their mar - ches. Wel - come, Welcome!

GREETING.

MT. LEBANON, N. Y.

We meet to bid you welcome, The an - gel bands are here, With - in our home—our precious home—To every heart so dear.

'Tis love in-spires the greet - ing, All joy-ous, warm and free, Like golden bil - lows meeting, Up - on the sum - mer sea.

We blend our hearts, and glad - ly come, To wel-come you to your loved home, Your own be - lov - ed home.

FAITH'S VISION.

MT. LEBANON, N. Y.

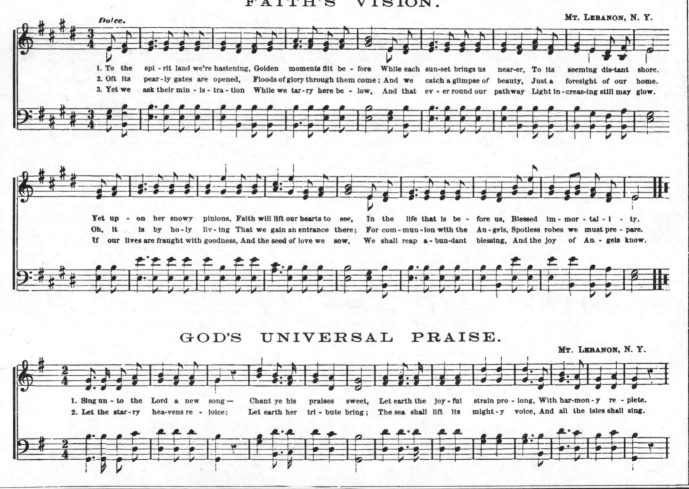

1. To the spi-rit land we're hastening, Golden moments flit be-fore While each sun-set brings us near-er, To its seeming dis-tant shore.
2. Oft its pear-ly gates are opened, Floods of glory through them come; And we catch a glimpse of beauty, Just a foresight of our home.
3. Yet we ask their min-is-tra-tion While we tar-ry here be-low, And that ev-er round our pathway Light in-creas-ing still may glow.

Yet up-on her snowy pinions, Faith will lift our hearts to see, In the life that is be-fore us, Blessed im-mor-tal-i-ty.
Oh, it is by ho-ly liv-ing That we gain an entrance there; For com-mun-ion with the An-gels, Spotless robes we must pre-pare.
If our lives are fraught with goodness, And the seed of love we sow, We shall reap a-bun-dant blessing, And the joy of An-gels know.

GOD'S UNIVERSAL PRAISE.

MT. LEBANON, N. Y.

1. Sing un-to the Lord a new song— Chant ye his praises sweet, Let earth the joy-ful strain pro-long, With har-mon-y re-plete.
2. Let the star-ry hea-vens re-joice; Let earth her tri-bute bring; The sea shall lift its might-y voice, And all the isles shall sing.

GOD'S UNIVERSAL PRAISE—Continued.

A - gain at - tune the heart-felt song, And bless His ho - ly name. Sal - va - tion doth to Him be - long, Let ev - 'ry voice pro - claim.

Green fields in gladness shall a - bound, And yield a rich in - crease, While for - ests shall with joy re - sound—The an-thems of sweet peace.

OUR ZION HOME.

MT. LEBANON, N. Y.

Tenderly.

1. We need no earth-ly flow - ers, To deck our Zi - on home, No ar - ti - fi - cial ra - di-ance, To light her sac-red dome; For an-gel gifts and gra - ces,

2. While transient pleasures per - ish, And fade as earthly flowers, Our joys are for e - ter - ni - ty, Our home in truth's fair bowers; Where heart to heart is blending,

A-dorn with beauty bright, And God's transcendent glo - ry, Her man - sion fills with light. O, Home, sweet Home! Blest joys are thine.

In pu - ri - ty and love, Where min-is-ters at - tend-ing, Re - new from spheres a - bove O, Home, sweet Home! Blest joys are thine.

HARPS OF WELCOME.

Joyously.

MT. LEBANON, N. Y.

We would greet our kindred true, and your life with strength re - new; Break ye waves of joy in mus - ic,

let the harps of wel - come ring! Love, re-joicing and thanksgiving, we with hap - py spi-rits bring; Many bless-ings

we're pos-sess-ing, these we free - ly would im - part. May the wealth of deep af - fec - tion bind more closely heart to heart;

Full

Oh, receive the love we bring, while the harps of wel-come ring! Oh, receive the love we bring, while the harps of wel-come ring.

GEM OF PEACE.

MT. LEBANON, N. Y.

1. With words of peace our friends we greet, And feel that ev' - ry heart, Hath some-thing good and pure and sweet—Of which we ask a part.
2. Oh, we will lift the bur-dens here, With hearts as true as steel; And toil with-in the Gos-pel sphere, For one an - o-ther's weal.

GEM OF PEACE—Continued.

We'll search for jew - els, ga - ther gems—Mid all the walks of life, To sparkle in our di - a-dems, When we have ceased the strife.

Un - wea - ried in the strength of love, Life's joys we will in - crease, And by our souls best ef - forts prove, We hold the gift of peace.

CHRISTMAS EVE.

MT. LEBANON, N. Y.

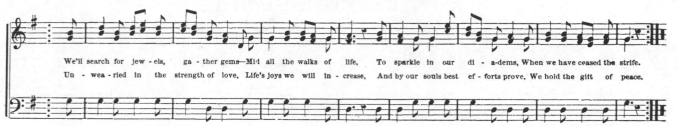

We have found the promised Saviour Who hath been so long fore-told; We have found the Christian goodness Which is worth a hun - dred fold.

And we'll spread the gladsome tid - ings, 'Till the sound of war shall cease; 'Till the homes of all are brightened— By the glorious Prince of peace.

Afetuoso.

And ere we meet the hour of slumber, Or breathe the last good-night, We'll softly whisper, sweet - ly sing In a cho-rus u - nite to kindred here, Peace! peace.

RETURNING SPRING.

MT. LEBANON, N. Y.

1. The voice of the re-turn-ing Spring Bids na-ture wake and rise; And put her best new garments on, For she has fresh sup-plies.

2. Then why should we, whose lines have fallen. In such a pleas-ant place, Be back-ward in the praise of Him, Or e'er fall short of grace?

3. We've all the eye of man could wish, And fruit-ful is the land; And greater than As-sy-rian hosts, The an-gels round us stand.

How wond'rous are the ways of God! How boun-ti-ful His hand! We see His love in ev'-ry tree, And broad-cast o'er the land.

We ought to leap, and shout, and sing, Till all the mountains round, Re-ver-be-rate the joy-ful news, To earth's re-mot-est bound.

And yet, to many thousands more, We such a home could give; If they would leave a car-nal world, And learn in Christ to live.

CHRISTMAS GREETING.

Mt Lebanon, N. Y.

Up - on this love - ly Christmas morning, We come forth our friends to cheer; In the East, the star is beaming; Lo! we've found the

Saviour near.   Oh, we love to spread the tid - ings, That will glad-den eve - ry heart; That with him we may be ris - ing,

Amoroso.

In his suffer - ing have a part.   Hark! I hear the an - gels sing - ing, Peace! peace on earth, good will to all.

VOYAGE OF LIFE

Mt. Lebanon, N. Y.

1. Up - on the rock - y shores of Time Our barques might anchored be, Yet pilot - like our spir - its long To cross life's rolling sea.
2. O, youthful mar - i - ner be-ware! Thy ves - sel frail may strand, Un-less 'tis guid-ed on its way By Truth's un-err-ing hand;

Repeat softly.

To sail ... a - way! .. Up - on its changeful tide, To brave the tempest and the storm, And o'er the bil - lows ride.
Then sail ... a - way! And leave all phan-tom fears. Prepare with strength to meet the flow Of the in - com - ing years.

3.
Though deep and strong the current glides,
Far out upon the sea,
Yet Faith—thy compass—will direct,
And Hope thy light will be;
    Still sail away!
Nor trust in thine own power,
But watch and pray though calm the day,
Or dark the midnight hour.

4.
The treasured wealth of patient toil,
Within thy spirit hold;
The shining pearls of Wisdom, place
Upon life's threads of gold.
    And sail away!
With Love at thy command,
To buoy thee up, and cheer the way,
To the immortal land.

5.
Thy finite vision cannot span,
Or bound the mighty deep;
The secrets of the future years,
Within its bosom sleep;
    But sail away!
O voyager on the main!
Within the blessed port of peace,
Sure anchorage thou wilt gain.

MILLENNIUM.

MT. LEBANON, N. Y.

HEAVENLY PATHWAY.

MT. LEBANON, N. Y.

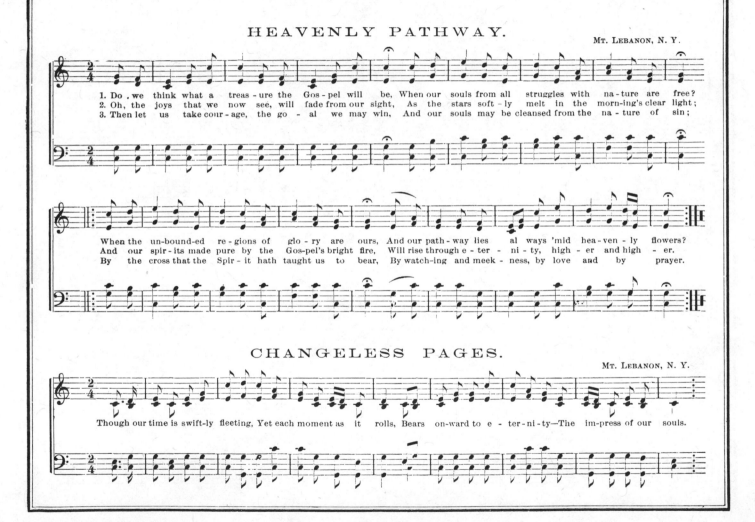

1. Do . we think what a treas - ure the Gos - pel will be, When our souls from all struggles with na - ture are free?
2. Oh, the joys that we now see, will fade from our sight, As the stars soft - ly melt in the morn-ing's clear light;
3. Then let us take cour - age, the go - al we may win, And our souls may be cleansed from the na - ture of sin;

When the un-bound-ed re - gions of glo - ry are ours, And our path - way lies al ways 'mid hea - ven - ly flowers?
And our spir - its made pure by the Gos-pel's bright fire, Will rise through e - ter - ni - ty, high - er and high - er.
By the cross that the Spir - it hath taught us to bear, By watch-ing and meek - ness, by love and by prayer.

CHANGELESS PAGES.

MT. LEBANON, N. Y.

Though our time is swift-ly fleeting, Yet each moment as it rolls, Bears on-ward to e - ter-ni-ty—The im-press of our souls.

CHANGELESS PAGES—Continued.

On our memories changeless pages, Shall our thoughts and actions stand, To bless, or blight the spir-it, In the im-mor-tal land.

"PEACE BE STILL."

MT. LEBANON, N. Y.

1. Peace, peace ye wild winds that shake the dark for - est! Be still ye fierce tem-pests that rock the great sea!
2. My soul shall be strong 'mid the wild storms of nature, And firm - ly my spir - it on God will de - pend.

Your strength is as weak-ness, com - pared with the pow - er Of those, who from bondage have set them-selves free.
Then, an - gels of light shall my dark path il - lu-mine, For God is my Fa-ther, my Mo - ther, and friend.

MISSION OF SONGS.

MT. LEBANON, N. Y.

1. Oh, when the songs of Zi - on Have reached, and touched your hearts, And Truth—the Ho - ly Spir - it— Its last - ing power im - parts.
2. The Daughter of Jer - usa - lem Has come to her stronghold, And Israel sits be - neath his vine, As Mi - cah's word fore-told.

Then may it teach how vain - ly The world would lure you on, And show to you the bles - sed path That no - ble souls have gone.
God's house of rev - e - la - tion Es - tab - lished on the hill, As - sem - bles those who hear the law, And its be - hests ful - fill.

For by the streams of Ba - by - lon, No more the cap-tives mourn, But from the ci - ty of our God, Sweet mel - o - dies are borne.

THE DEPENDENCE OF THE SINGING OR SPEAKING FORM OF THE LARYNX UPON THE RESPIRATORY EFFORT.

THE TWO FORMS, THE TWO BREATHS, THE TWO LOCALITIES OF TONE.

Before entering upon the main argument, the reader is requested to go through with the following exercises; for the real import and vital importance of the subject will be more vividly realized if every statement can be at once submitted to the crucial test of a personal trial. In all the standard treatises on physiology (*vide* Flint, Dalton, and Carpenter), the respiratory movement of the glottis is fully described; its relation to singing or speaking, as a natural law which should be recognized as of superlative importance in restoring or educating the voice, is claimed by the writer as an original discovery.

Ex. 1. *Inflate the lungs by an effort of the muscles which expand the chest and raise the shoulders, then expel the breath by simply relaxing this effort.*

The weight of the unnaturally elevated and distended chest is amply sufficient to discharge the newly inhaled air; but mark these two related facts — the breathing was effortless, the breath was shrilly audible.

Ex. 2. *Contract the abdominal muscles steadily and powerfully —in other words, draw inward the abdomen by regular degrees, to expel the breath; but be watchful to avoid an involuntary expansion of the chest.*

If the abdomen is drawn inward, the lungs will be compressed; and, if the chest is not allowed to expand, the air must be driven out through the windpipe, but so noiselessly will it escape, that its flow will be almost imperceptible. And now take notice again — the breathing was attended by a decided effort; the breath was almost or quite inaudible.

It is a curious fact, remarked upon at some length by Dr. Flint, that a person who feels that he is the subject of an experiment, will unconsciously disturb the natural respiratory process, and the reader will be very likely to associate breathing with the sound of issuing breath so strongly, that the respiration in the second, as well as the first exercise, will be plainly heard.

To avoid this danger by a simple stratagem, let the thought concern itself solely with the abdominal effort. The breath will then be discharged through the mouth so noiselessly (unless the flow of air is very great), that it will require some test, such as holding the hand before the mouth, to reveal that it is indeed flowing. If this muscular effort cannot at once be determined, let two or three short coughs rapidly succeed each other, while great care is taken to so far depart from the natural habit of coughing that a preliminary breath will not be drawn, nor the chest convulsively expand. In this way the abdominal effort will be plainly indicated, and with a little practice, the second exercise can be fairly performed.

There are then two distinct breaths — which may be designated as the rushing and the flooding breaths; and the great difference in their rate of flow, while the respiratory effort remains unchanged, proves that the capacity of the duct through which they flow, cannot have remained the same. The noisier current of the former rushing breath can be explained only by supposing that the channel is narrower; the noiseless passage and more rapid flow of the flooding breath certainly indicate a wider outlet.

But the laryngeal cavity cannot be changed without altering the form of the larynx. There must then be two distinct forms of the larynx, each assumed naturally, without the aid of the forcing muscles previously noticed, whose contraction would be distinctly felt and recognized. By what agency, then, is the change effected?

Happily, the study of physiology has found the true and wonderful solution of this difficult problem in the involuntary *respiratory movement of the glottis.*

Physiology has discovered that in man, and in all the higher animals, the laryngeal cavity actively enlarges from one-fifth to one-third when the breath is inhaled, but passively collapses to its former state when it is exhaled. No one can fail to notice how differently the two breaths sound of a person in sleep. At the first thought, it must appear that this involuntary habit would directly oppose the use of the wider form by the vocalist, for in singing the breath is exhaled.

But this widening and narrowing does not depend upon the direction of the breath inward or outward, but results from the sympathy between the respiratory muscles and the pair of laryngeal muscles, which contract to widen the opening. Hence, in ordinary breathing (as was shown by the first exercise), the muscles of the larynx contract during inspiration in response to the breathing muscles, which must contract to raise the chest or lower the diaphragm; but in expiration they relax, because they have no respiratory effort to sympathize with—for the breathing muscles relax to let the chest or diaphragm recoil to their natural position with a force fully adequate to expel to breath.

And that the direction of the breath is not important, but that the laryngeal muscles always contract, or strive to contract, whenever the respiratory muscles are exerted for whatever purpose, the softer flow of the breath, when it is expelled by a decided effort of the abdominal muscles (as in the 2d exercise), convincingly proves.

But are not the respiratory muscles exerted in speaking and singing? The simple recoil of the chest sufficed to expel the breath when the larnyx is open; but in speaking or singing, it is closed by the vocal chords, so that for even a moderate tone, the air must be propelled with greater force, and the respiratory muscles actually exert themselves. Space forbids an express statement of the various demands made upon these muscles by the exigencies of the musical tone or phrase; and it would require too long a process of reasoning to show why the faintest note for which the mere rebound of the chest would be sufficient and more than sufficient motive power, should depend instead upon a positive effort of both the abdominal muscles and the diaphragm. For they should contract in opposition to each other—the lower muscles bearing upward, the diaphragm downward, with a slight overbalance of force in favor of the former; a combined effort entirely disproportionate to the vocal effect produced. So far we must beg the question, resting our opinion upon good authorities. But that dependence is not placed upon the simple recoil, is shown by the strange and unnaturally husky tone which a person speaks when he raises his shoulders and expands the chest, and talks while they listlessly rebound to their normal position; the force will be adequate, but the sound shows that some natural law has been violated.

This law reads as follows: *The singing or speaking breath should always be impelled by a positive effort of the respiratory muscles.*

Such is the law; but when it is disobeyed, and the singing breath is discharged without effort, why is the tone impaired? What is the wanting condition which the respiratory effort supplies? It cannot be found in the different impulse given to the breath; for the simple recoil impels it in the same direction, and for a moderate tone, with sufficient force. The conclusion cannot be avoided that the channel is changed for the vocalized air, by the pair of laryngeal muscles which act in sympathy with the respiratory muscles.

This natural law of vocalizing may be formulated as follows: *The singing form of the larynx depends primarily upon an effort of the laryngeal muscles of dilation (the crico-arytenoidei postici); secondarily, upon the positive exertion of the respiratory muscles.*

It may be reasonably supposed that the two powerful muscles of dilation must have an influence, if they are exerted while the other vocal muscles make tense and approximate the vocal chords; but to explain exactly how they operate, will require a brief sketch of the vocal organs.

The vocal chords stretch horizontally across the larynx, or top of the windpipe, from the front backward. At the front, they come close together, but as they extend backward, they diverge like the two sides of the letter "V." If the first and second finger are stretched apart, and the neck is set in the fork, the position and divergence of the chords will be roughly, but on too large a scale, indicated.

At the back of the larynx they are attached to two movable cartilages, somewhat in the form of pyramids, called the arytenoid cartilages, to which are also attached the vocal chords. But these pyramids are also the support of the two epiglottidean muscles which draw inward folds of the mucous membrane just above the vocal chords, when the throat must be closed for an explosive cough, or in swallowing. Now, the vocal chords and vocal muscles (including the sympathetic dilating muscles) are all attached to the base of the pyramids, while the epiglottidean muscles are fastened at their apex. When the muscles of dilation contract, they pull upon the outer angle of the base of each pyramid, drawing this angle outward and downward: their outward pulling would draw apart the basis of the pyramid; their downward pulling would tip them out of the perpendicular, so that their summits would be farther apart than their bases.

When the vocal chords must come together for speaking or singing, the muscles of approximation (the arytenoideus and crico-arytenoidei laterales) contract to draw the pyramids together, still in this slanting position. The vocal chords will come close together at the base; but, as the dilating muscles are still active, the sides will incline away from each other, and afford an ever-widening space to the newly vocalized air, whose vibratory waves will be unbroken in their passage to the pharynx and mouth. But if the respiratory effort did not prompt the dilating laryngeal muscles to incline the pyramidal supports outward, their sides, as well as base, would come nearer together; the aperture from the base to the apex, or entrance to the mouth, would be narrow; the vocal waves would be broken, and the resulting tone husky and impure.

And as no theory in art is valuable until it is reduced to practice, let this newly acquired knowledge be utilized by being thrown into the form of exercises. Its enormous training value to the student will at once be recognized.

Ex. 3. *Exhale the breath as in Ex.* 1, *by a simple recoil. Repeat this breath, but midway decide that the latter half shall carry out a tone with it, but avoid any change of physical effort.*

That is, avoid any effort other than the respiratory, which must remain unchanged. The thought of a coming tone will indeed prompt the vocal muscles to action, but they are utterly devoid of sensation, and the scholar's only solicitude need be to avoid any physical effort, or any feeling whatever in the throat. In this exercise, the tone will sound like a sigh and will lack resonance; the air will flow almost as fast in the tone as in the toneless breath.

Ex. 4. *Exhale the breath as in Ex.* 2, *with a decided effort, and with a noiseless current, but just as soon as the hand held before the mouth shows that a strong current of air is setting outward, introduce the tone with the same solicitude to avoid the slightest change of physical effort.* Strictly performed, this exercise will evolve a tone of the last degree of excellence — a tone so pure and so resonant that it will show that every particle of air has been vocalized to its utmost capacity.

This series of exercises carries with it its own sufficient proof, and can, from the first, be practiced with good results. But the laborious distention of the chest may soon be dispensed with, if the exact sound of the rushing breath is kept well in remembrance; for such voluntary control will have been acquired that the narrower form of the larynx can be assumed, even when the breath is expelled by a positive exertion of the abdominal muscles — an effort according more nearly with the mode of respiration upon which the cultivated artist or speaker should rely.

Even when a clear note can be made to enter after the soft breath in the middle of the compass of his voice, the scholar must not stop practicing with the rushing breath; for it will soon appear that the muscles of pitch can, with this form of the larynx, far more easily learn to stretch the now untrammeled chords for a high pitch, in response to the sheer mental projection of the note — an unwonted effort requiring that they shall learn new habits, for now they have dissolved partnership with the disturbing epiglottidean muscles, and must perform the whole office alone.

And the zealous student may well be cheered and stimulated, when he finds that he is accomplishing in months the accustomed labor of years; that at the bottom of this unpromising solution of husky sound and fatiguing practice are being crystallized the precious jewels of oratory and song — tones clear cut, transparent and beautiful, whose transmitted light, softly diffused in many varying tints and shades, will faithfully portray the otherwise inexpressible emotions to which he would give utterance.

JOHN HOWARD.

ERRATA.

At all the repeats there should be a double bar.

In "Home of Peace," (p. 20), where there are two parts only it should be marked Duet, and where there are three, Trio.

"Glad New Year," (p. 21), in first verse "true" should be full.

"Triumph," (p. 23), the staves should not be braced.

"Welcome," (p. 24), the two first staves should not be braced.

"Times of Refreshing," (p. 24), the staves should not be braced.

"New Year's Greeting," (p. 29), the last line of second verse should be indented.

"Come to Zion," (p. 38), the notes to the word "sea," should be semiquaver and dotted quaver.

"Blessings," (p. 31), the signature is omitted in the second bass staff.

"Morning Dawn," (p. 39), the note under the last "the" in the chorus should be quavered.

"Spirit of Truth," (p. 40), the note to the first syllable of "immortal" should be D, and the note to the word "fail" should be D.

"Farewell," (p. 44), the last bass note to the last syllable of "scattered" should be in the first space.

"Power of Love," (p. 48), the tenor note to the last syllable of "purified" should be on the fourth line of the staff.

"A Chant," (p. 49), $\frac{4}{4}$ should be at the beginning, and barred accordingly.

"All is Summer," (p. 50), "wing" should be wings.

"Greeting," (p. 53), the sharp in the alto should be a natural.

"Gem of Peace," (p. 56), the repeat should be after the rest.

"Millennium," (p. 61), the last two bars should retard.

"Changeless Pages," (p. 62), the third alto note from the end should be on the leger line, and the last note stemmed down.

CONTENTS.